W9-BLA-317

Linking art to the world around us

Arty Facts

Animals
& Art Activities

Crabtree Publishing Company
www.crabtreebooks.com

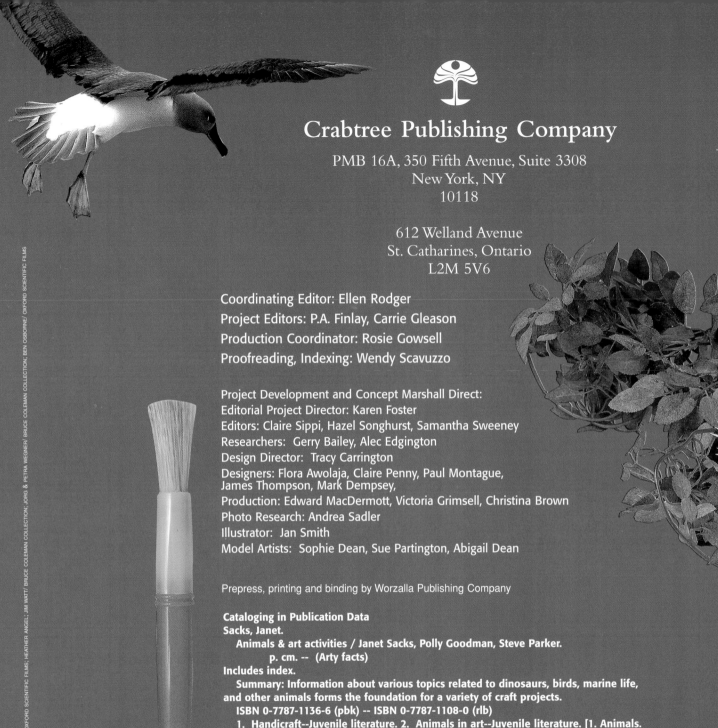

Crabtree Publishing Company

PMB 16A, 350 Fifth Avenue, Suite 3308
New York, NY
10118

612 Welland Avenue
St. Catharines, Ontario
L2M 5V6

Coordinating Editor: Ellen Rodger
Project Editors: P.A. Finlay, Carrie Gleason
Production Coordinator: Rosie Gowsell
Proofreading, Indexing: Wendy Scavuzzo

Project Development and Concept Marshall Direct:
Editorial Project Director: Karen Foster
Editors: Claire Sippi, Hazel Songhurst, Samantha Sweeney
Researchers: Gerry Bailey, Alec Edgington
Design Director: Tracy Carrington
Designers: Flora Awolaja, Claire Penny, Paul Montague,
James Thompson, Mark Dempsey,
Production: Edward MacDermott, Victoria Grimsell, Christina Brown
Photo Research: Andrea Sadler
Illustrator: Jan Smith
Model Artists: Sophie Dean, Sue Partington, Abigail Dean

Prepress, printing and binding by Worzalla Publishing Company

Cataloging in Publication Data
Sacks, Janet.
   Animals & art activities / Janet Sacks, Polly Goodman, Steve Parker.
        p. cm. -- (Arty facts)
Includes index.
   Summary: Information about various topics related to dinosaurs, birds, marine life,
and other animals forms the foundation for a variety of craft projects.
   ISBN 0-7787-1136-6 (pbk) -- ISBN 0-7787-1108-0 (rlb)
   1. Handicraft--Juvenile literature. 2. Animals in art--Juvenile literature. [1. Animals.
2. Handicraft.] I. Title: Animals and art activities. II. Goodman, Polly. III. Parker, Steve.
IV. Title. V. Series.
   TT160 .S173 2002
   745.5--dc21   2002000350
                                                                  LC

Created by
Marshall Direct Learning

© 2002 Marshall Direct Learning

FRONT COVER IMAGES: NORBERT ROSING/ OXFORD SCIENTIFIC FILMS; HEATHER ANGEL, JIM WATT/ BRUCE COLEMAN COLLECTION; JORG & PETRA WEGNER/ BRUCE COLEMAN COLLECTION; BEN OSBORNE/ OXFORD SCIENTIFIC FILMS

Linking art to the world around us

Arty Facts

Animals
& Art Activities

Contents

WRITTEN BY Janet Sacks, Polly Goodman, Steve Parker

Dinosaurs

A model of a baby parasaurolophus hatching out of an egg.

Carnivores

Some dinosaurs were gigantic, fearsome hunters with large mouths, massive teeth, and curving claws. The tyrannosaurus rex was 40 feet (12 m) long, with an enormous head. The giganotosaurus was even bigger – as long as 43 feet (13 m), with a mouth the size of a small car. The compsognathus was chicken-sized and darted around hunting small animals.

Giants

The diplodocus and brachiosaurus were herbivores, or plant-eaters. They were nearly twice as long as a transport truck, and more than twice as heavy. The maiasauras guarded their eggs in a nest scooped out of the soil. They brought their **hatchlings** berries, leaves, and plants to eat, and protected them from hungry **predators**.

No survivors

The Age of Dinosaurs spanned from about 230 million to 65 million years ago. Then, suddenly, the dinosaurs all died out. No one really knows why. Many scientists believe that Earth was hit by a giant lump of rock from outer space called an asteroid. The asteroid caused a massive explosion and dust cloud that brought years of cold and darkness, killing all the dinosaurs. Some close relatives of the dinosaurs are living today – birds, and **reptiles**, such as crocodiles.

M illions of years ago, in prehistoric times, giant **dinosaurs** lived on the Earth. They were some of the biggest, fastest, and fiercest animals there has ever been. They lived in all parts of the world, in many different surroundings. They ate every kind of food, and some even ate each other!

Animals

Model dinorama

colored Plasticine

poster board

paints and brush

stick

2 Use the stick to add patterns and texture to the Plasticine.

1 Shape your Plasticine to create a collection of dinosaurs.

Make a leafy prehistoric scene to put your dinosaurs in

3 Paint a leafy scene on white poster board to make a backdrop for your dinosaurs.

Showing off!

Many birds in the **rainforests** of South America and on tropical Pacific islands **display** very bright, colorful feathers. Their feathers are a natural work of art, but they have a practical purpose as well. Bright feathers help the male bird to attract a female during the **mating** season.

Birds of paradise

The bird of paradise is one of the most beautiful birds in the world. There are more than 40 different varieties, and most of these live on the tropical island of New Guinea. They live in forests, where they feed on fruits and insects. Before the mating season, the male birds gather in trees to display their brightly colored feathers to the dull-colored females. Their **plumage** grows in many strange forms and colors. Birds of paradise strut and dance and spread out their feathers so that they can be more easily seen.

Greater bird of paradise

The greater bird of paradise is one of the most exotically plumed birds in the world. Its forehead and throat are emerald green, its head is golden yellow, and its wings and tail are maroon. From under its wings sprout dense feathers about two feet (61 cm) long.

Courtship

The males perform a mating dance, or courtship display. After the female has chosen a mate, she builds a nest and lays up to three eggs in it.

A beautiful tropical bird with bright red plumage.

Animals

WHAT YOU NEED

pencil

toilet paper rolls

scissors

egg carton

colored paper

wire

glue

tape

construction paper

tissue paper

1 Cut a small section from the toilet paper roll. Cut a beak shape from the egg carton and wedge it into the smaller roll.

2 Glue the smaller part of the roll on top of the larger section to make the bird's head.

3 Use wire to make two legs with feet. Poke the legs through the base of the body. Bend them so that the bird stands firmly. Tape them in place.

4 Cut strips of colored paper. Twist them around a pencil to make curly tail feathers.

5 Cut more strips to make a fringe and glue this around the body.

How many colors will your bird have?

6 Cut two wings out of construction paper and glue them to each side of the bird. Decorate the wings with strips of colored paper.

You can add real feathers too!

7 Scrunch up tissue paper into small balls and cover the throat and head of your bird.

Patches and stripes

The **animal kingdom** is a stunning display of skin patterns and colors. Male peacocks use their dazzling patterns to attract a mate. For zebras, tigers, giraffes, and many other animals, their patterns are more than just a fashion display or an opportunity to show off. They are a matter of life or death.

Hidden hunters

Tigers live in the forests and tall grasslands of Asia. Their orange-and-black stripes let them move almost unseen, while stealthily stalking an antelope or deer. Without its **camouflage** and hunting skills, the tiger would starve. The pattern on each tiger is unique – no other tiger's pattern is exactly the same.

Safe in the shade

A giraffe's coat has a patchy brown pattern. Standing among the trees in the dappled sunlight, giraffes can be surprisingly difficult to see. While feeding, they need to stay as hidden from prowling lions as possible.

Spot the herd

Each zebra's black-and-white striped coat is unique. The different patterns help zebras recognize their own **herd** among the many others that roam the grassy plains. The safest place for zebras to be is in the herd. The more ears listening for an approaching lion, the better the chance the herd has to gallop away.

Zebra mask

1 Put a piece of white poster board up to your face and mark where your eyes are.

2 Draw the outline of a zebra's face and cut it out.

3 Paint black stripes onto the zebra face.

4 Cut out two circles for the eyes and two for the nostrils. Cut out a tuft of hair from black paper and glue it on.

5 Attach the bamboo stick onto the back of the zebra's face with tape. Your mask is now ready to hold up to your face.

Make a collection of other animal masks

9

Super scales

Fish and reptiles, such as snakes and lizards, are covered with flat plates called scales. These small, hard scales protect the animal's soft body. Turtles and crocodiles have large, bony, armor-like plates instead of scales. The pangolin is the only **mammal** with scales. It looks like a big pine cone with legs!

Sharp or smooth

Some fish have thin, bony scales with rounded edges, but the way the scales lie on their bodies actually makes them smooth to touch. Other fish have scales with tiny, sharp points on the surface, so they feel rough. A shark's skin looks very smooth, but is covered with overlapping scales that look like tiny teeth.

Most predators cannot break through the scaly skin of a pangolin.

Second skin

Snakes have dry, overlapping scales. They even have clear scales over their eyes. Several times a year, a new scaly skin grows under the old one. The snake wiggles out of its worn skin head-first, rubbing itself against rocks to help get the old skin off.

Body armor

A turtle's shell has two layers of bony plates. The inner layer is part of the **skeleton**. Horny, joined plates called **scutes** make up the outer layer. Armadillos are small mammals with bony plates that slide over each other, so they can move easily. If a predator gets too close, the armadillo rolls up tightly into a hard, bony ball.

Animals

Wiggly snake

1 Cut some wide strips of construction paper. Fold them in half lengthwise and tape down one edge as shown.

2 Draw and cut out enough oval shapes to make a long snake.

3 Poke holes in each end of the ovals and use paper fasteners to join them together.

Make a scaly snake family

4 Make a triangular-shaped tail from construction paper and fasten it to one end of the snake's body.

5 Glue two beads onto the head for eyes. Make a tongue with the pipe cleaner and decorate the body with colored sequins.

Best nests

The most important jobs in building a nest are finding the right materials and putting them together in the right way. A bird's nest can be a simple hollow in the ground, or a fantastic, woven, hanging structure. Male bowerbirds build a nest and decorate it with all the bright objects they can find – colorful flowers, berries, shells, foil, or plastic. They replace the materials as the colors fade.

Cup shapes

To make a cup-shaped nest, the bird sits in the middle of all the materials it has collected and turns around in circles, pushing outward until the shape is right. Hummingbirds make the smallest cup-shaped nests – they are only one and a half inches (4 cm) across!

Weavers

If a male weaver bird wants to impress a mate, his nest must be the best! Weavers tie complicated knots with their beaks and feet. A nest starts as a hanging ring. By looping, twisting, and knotting strips of leaves, the bird then weaves the ring into a round hollow nest. Sometimes, a long entrance tunnel is added to keep snakes out.

Animals

Make a fluffy bird to sit on your nest

WHAT YOU NEED

wire mesh

eggs

needle

brush

paints

feathers

bowl

paper

hay or dried grass

1 Create a nest shape with the wire mesh.

Using feathers, hay, grass, and twisted strips of paper, weave in and out of the mesh to create the nest.

2

3 Use the needle to make a hole at each end of the eggs. Blow out the inside of the eggs into a bowl as shown. Paint speckles on the eggs and place them in the nest.

13

Warm and woolly

Many animals have thick, furry coats to keep them warm in winter. When the weather starts to get warm, many animals molt, or shed their coats. We use this unwanted **fur** or wool to make clothes for ourselves.

Sheep's fleece

The fur we use most comes from sheep. In warmer weather, farmers cut off, or shear, the sheep's heavy coats with electric clippers. The fleece is then sent to a factory. At the factory, the fleece, or raw wool, is cleaned and spun into thread, called yarn. There are two types of yarn: woolen and worsted. The fine threads, or fibers, of woolen yarn are messy. In worsted, the fibers are combed flat. Worsted yarn is used to make smooth cloth.

Soft and silky

An angora rabbit has very long fur. When loose fur is combed from its coat and mixed with wool, it makes a soft, fluffy yarn. We also get soft, fluffy, mohair wool from the long, silky coats of angora goats.

Costly cashmere

The softest, most luxurious wool of all is called cashmere, or pashmina. It comes from the downy undercoat of the Kashmir goat found in mountainous regions of Asia. During the molting season, the fur is combed out by hand. One cashmere sweater uses fur from four to five goats, and a long coat takes thirty to forty fleeces. No wonder cashmere clothes are so expensive!

Animals

Fluffy sheep

Glue a stick fence around your patchwork field

variety of textured
paper

cotton balls

gluestick

paints
and brush

scissors   poster
board

sticks

white
paper

1 Glue cotton balls onto a piece of paper. Paint some black and some white. Cut out when dry.

2 On white paper, draw the legs and heads of the sheep and cut them out.

3 Create a patchwork field by gluing squares of colored and textured paper onto your poster board.

4 Glue legs and heads onto the cotton balls. Now glue your sheep onto the patchwork field.

15

Sponge shapes

Did you know that the natural sponge you use in the bath is actually a living sea animal? Sponges live on rocks deep in the ocean. They are collected by deep-sea divers. Before they are sold, the living parts are removed and the sponge is cleaned, leaving the soft, spongy skeleton.

Strange sea animal

A sponge is not like any other living animal. A sponge does not even have a mouth! A sponge's body is filled with tiny holes, so water flows through it. Very tiny plants and animals in the water, called **plankton**, get trapped inside the sponge and are eaten.

Big and small

There are more than 5,000 different kinds of sponges. The biggest are seven feet (2 m), while the smallest are only about one inch (2 cm) long.

Useful sponges

People have used sponges for thousands of years. Greek and Roman soldiers padded their helmets and armor with them, and even drank from them. Today, we use sponges for cleaning things, as protective padding, and even for painting walls! Now we usually use **synthetic** sponges, so the natural sponges are left alone to grow in peace.

Animals

WHAT YOU NEED

white paper

paints

poster board

scissors

paintbrush

glue

toothpicks

sponge

Make colorful sponge pictures to hang on your bedroom wall

1 Mix colored paint with the glue.

2 Paint the mixture onto pieces of paper. Scratch patterns with a toothpick. Leave to dry.

3 Cut pieces of sponge into several shapes.

4 Paint the sponge shapes with different colors. Print them onto your textured surfaces. When dry, mount your pictures on poster board.

17

Spines and prickles

How do animals protect themselves from a hungry predator? One way is to have a spiky coat. If the animal cannot run very fast, it can stay still and use its spikes for **defense**. An animal covered in sharp spikes can protect itself from the fiercest predator.

Spiky back

The porcupine's back is covered in a double layer of long, black-and-white **quills**. When frightened, it rattles its quills to make them stand up and stamps its feet. If this does not scare away the predator, the porcupine rushes backwards at it. Sometimes, part of a quill is left in the other animal's skin.

Prickly ball

A **hedgehog's** coat of spikes only grows on the upper part of its body. The rest is covered in coarse hair. When a hedgehog is frightened, it rolls up. Its soft back part, head, and feet are tucked up safely into a prickly ball.

Spiky skins

The stickleback is a small fish that lives mainly in fresh water. When threatened, spikes on its back and tail lock upright. A predator gets a mouthful of spikes that are almost impossible to swallow. One family of sea animals is called **echinodermata**, which means "prickly skinned animals." It includes starfish and spiky sea urchins.

Animals

Spiky porcupine

WHAT YOU NEED

clay

beads or buttons

toothpicks

leafy stems

1 Roll the clay into a ball and form a snout at one end.

2 Use two beads or buttons for the eyes.

3 Stick the toothpicks into the clay all over the body.

4 Scratch on the nose and facial markings with a toothpick.

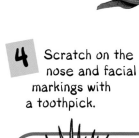

Make a leafy home for your porcupine!

19

Pouches and pockets

Marsupials are animals that have pockets, called **pouches,** in their skin. Kangaroos, koalas, and opossums are all marsupials. They use their pouches as safe places for their babies to grow. The koala's pouch is on its back, but kangaroos and opossums have pouches in front.

Safe inside

When a young marsupial is born, its eyes, ears, and back legs are not yet formed. Blind, deaf, and unable to walk for the first six or seven weeks, the baby needs to be protected from the outside world.

Joey

When a baby kangaroo, or **joey**, is born it crawls into its mother's pouch. This can take as long as five hours. Once inside, the joey finds one of its mother's four milk-giving teats and holds on by its mouth. It stays there for about eight months, only leaving the pouch when it is big enough to hop around.

Clinging koala

Koalas live in trees, so the female's pouch is on her back. The newborn koala crawls inside and stays there for seven months. When it comes out, the baby clings to its mother's back for another six to twelve months, until it is ready to set out on its own.

Animals

WHAT YOU NEED

scissors

material

needle and thread

yarn

safety pin

sequins

1 Cut a circle and a long, wide strip from your piece of material.

2 Sew the long strip together as shown.

3 Follow the picture to sew the circular piece of material to the long strip.

4 Create pockets by cutting out different pieces of material and then sewing them onto the sides of the bag.

5 Turn the bag inside out. Fold over the top edge of the bag and sew it down, leaving a gap.

6 To make the drawstrings, tie yarn onto a safety pin and push it into the gap. Thread the pin through the top seam of the bag. Draw out both ends and pull to close.

Make a matching wallet or purse to go with your bag

Sew or glue sequins onto the pockets, or use embroidery thread to decorate your bag.

Snapping jaws

If you want to find out what kind of food an animal eats, look at its teeth and jaws. They are specially made to suit its diet. Plant-eaters such as deer have broad, flat teeth for grinding up grass. Alligators, sharks, and other meat-eaters have razor-sharp teeth for tearing and ripping flesh. Animals that eat both plants and meat have both kinds of teeth.

Shark attack!

Sharks swim through the oceans, hunting for food without ever stopping. When they attack, their powerful jaws bite and their long, jagged teeth slice, killing **prey** in minutes. A shark's enormous jaws can open so wide it can swallow prey whole. It uses its razor-sharp teeth to tear off chunks of flesh. They grow in rows inside the mouth, and new teeth replace the old, worn-down teeth as often as once a week. Sharks usually hunt and eat other fish – it is rare that they attack people.

Alligator roll

Crocodiles and alligators have long, snapping jaws full of sharp, strong teeth. They live in shallow lakes, slowly moving rivers, and swamps. They stay out of sight below the water's surface, waiting for an animal such as an antelope or a deer to come close enough. They then rush at their victim, grab it in their powerful jaws, and drag it into the water. Holding it tightly, they kill their prey by rolling around with it under water until it drowns.

Animals

Alligator arm mask

1 Draw, in two parts, an outline of an alligator's head on the poster board. Cut it out carefully.

2 Paint each part of your mask green.

3 Use strips of construction paper to make rings to fit around your arms, and tape them to the back of each part of the alligator's head.

4 Place on each arm and make snapping movements.

What other animals with snapping jaws can you make?

Danger signals

If you see a small, brightly colored animal – beware! Many small animals use bright colors for protection. The colors warn hungry predators that the animals are probably **poisonous**. Other small animals have patterns on their bodies that are meant to warn, startle, or fool predators.

Warning wings

Birds are the main predators of butterflies and moths. The insects must frighten away the birds, or be eaten. A monarch butterfly's bright, warning colors are a signal to keep birds away. The butterfly's body contains chemicals that will make a bird sick if it is eaten. A harmless insect that mimics, or looks similar to another harmful insect, uses a defense called **mimicry**. The harmless viceroy butterfly is the same color as the poisonous monarch butterfly, so birds avoid it too.

Hidden stings

Bees and wasps have bright yellow and black-and-white bodies to warn predators to beware of their sting. The wasp beetle, found in Europe, looks exactly like a wasp, so enemies leave it alone as well. Beetles such as ladybugs also use their colors and patterns to defend themselves.

Poison frogs

Many frogs produce **poison** from glands in their skin, so they are not eaten. The poison-dart frogs that live in the rainforests of Central and South America produce some of the most powerful poisons ever found. Their jewel-like color and patterns send a clear message to predators – stay away!

Animals

Fierce face mask

WHAT YOU NEED

2 small plastic containers

string

poster board

pipe cleaner

paints and brush

scissors

sequins

tissue paper

glue

silver and gold paints

1 Glue overlapping strips of tissue paper to the outside of the containers. Decorate with sequins and gold and silver paints.

2 Cut a slit in the top of each container. On poster board, draw and cut out two side panels for the containers and decorate.

3 Fold the straight edge and glue a panel to each container. Join the two containers together with a pipe cleaner. The pipe cleaner should fit over your nose.

Frighten your friends with horror headgear!

4 Make a spiked headband. Decorate and paint it.

5 Attach string to the headband and goggles. Tie the ends around your head. You are now wearing your fierce face mask!

You could also color the rest of your face with face paint.

25

Up and away

Perfect shape

Birds' wings are not all exactly the same shape. The woodpecker has short, rounded wings, so that it can turn quickly in forests with many trees. Pheasants have broad wings, so they can take off straight up into the air. The swift stays in the air for most of its life, flying at around 25 miles per hour (40 km/h). It only lands to mate and to lay eggs. Its slender, curved, pointed wings are ideal for non-stop flying. They lift the swift upward and are slim enough to cut through the air, keeping the bird from slowing down.

Super soarers

Most large birds soar and glide using the power of the wind to keep them up. Heavy **birds of prey** soar upwards on **thermals**. They ride on these columns of warm, rising air and only flap their wings to move from one thermal to another. A sea gull's long, pointed wings help it to glide on currents of air that bounce up from cliffs.

Hoverbird

To stay in one place in the air, a bird has to beat its wings continuously. Most birds can hover for only a short time. The bird that can hover for the longest is the kestrel. It beats its wings rapidly, but needs a slight wind to keep it up. The world's fastest flying bird is the peregrine falcon. It can dive to catch prey at an amazing 175 miles per hour (280 km/h)!

Have you ever watched a bird soaring through the air and wished that you could fly too? Birds' wings are shaped specially for flying. They are curved on top and slightly flatter underneath, so the air flowing over and under them lifts the bird into the air.

Animals

Swirly pictures

WHAT YOU NEED

paper

poster board

brushes

gluestick

feathers

glitter

paints

1 Using brushes and feathers, create a series of swooping strokes on your paper with paint.

2 Cut out your patterns and mount them on poster board.

3 Decorate some of them with glitter.

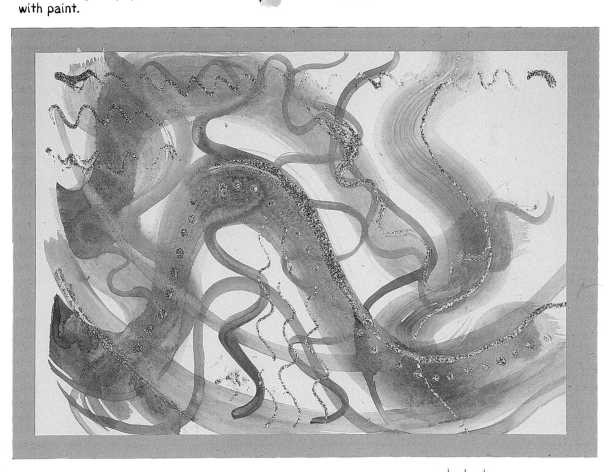

What else can you use to make unusual patterns and strokes?

27

Swing high!

Monkeys are real animal acrobats! They leap and swing through the treetops of their forest home. They balance, steer, and grip with their long, strong tails. Apes look very similar to monkeys, but are bigger, with longer arms, larger brains, and no tail. Apes and monkeys belong to the **primate** animal family, which also includes humans.

High life

Most monkeys spend their lives in the treetops. They find plenty of food there – fruit, nuts, and insects. Monkeys' bodies are ideal for living in and moving through the trees. They are slim and strong, with long arms, muscled legs, and long, curling fingers and toes. Monkeys have thumbs, so they can grip and hold things. They can even hang from a branch by their tails! When two monkeys rest together, they often hold tails to show they are friends.

Apes

Orangutans, gorillas, and chimpanzees are all apes. Apes are better climbers than monkeys, who prefer running and jumping. Apes also spend more time on the ground and walk more upright than monkeys. Like almost all primates, apes live together in close family groups.

Animals

Jungle monkeys

WHAT YOU NEED

poster board

paints and brush

yarn or string

colored pencils

scissors

pencil

1 Draw different monkeys onto the poster board, making sure the arms and tails curl, so the monkeys can hang from each other.

2 Cut them out and paint them different colors. When they are dry, use colored pencils to add detail.

Hang the monkeys from the leaves of a potted plant jungle

You can also make a monkey mobile. Attach string to one monkey and hang the rest from each other by their arms and tails.

Color-changer

A chameleon is an interesting animal. Its toes are joined together so that it can wrap its v-shaped feet tightly around branches. It has cone-shaped eyes that can swivel all the way around to spot its prey. As for changing color, a chameleon is the best!

Trickster

Most people think that a chameleon changes color to match its background, but its natural color is green or brown, so it already blends in with the forest. Its skin color makes it difficult to see and helps it to hide from predators. If a chameleon is seen, it has some tricks for escaping, such as flattening itself to look like part of a branch.

A chameleon can also puff itself up and open its mouth wide to hiss. If this doesn't work, it may drop off its branch onto the forest floor, where it will be hidden again.

Color-making cells

A chameleon's color changes as the light and temperature around it change. It also changes color when it is angry or scared. There are three layers of color cells in the chameleon's skin. The tiny, color-making parts inside the cells move to turn the chameleon different colors, even bright shades of yellow and red. Male chameleons often turn a bright color to attract a female.

Animals

Chameleon art

WHAT YOU NEED

colored
construction
paper

gluestick

pipe
cleaners

tissue paper

scissors

sequins

pencil

sticks

straws

1 Draw an outline of a
chameleon on a piece
of green construction
paper and cut it out –
head, body, and legs.

2 Decorate your chameleon
with small pieces of tissue
paper rolled into balls, straws
cut into small circles, and
sequins.

3 Glue these onto
your chameleon.

4 Use a pipe cleaner
to outline the mouth.

5 Glue the chameleon
on another piece of
construction paper
and glue the sticks underneath
its feet.

6 Glue on a brightly
colored pipe cleaner to
make the chameleon's
long, curly tongue.

31

Coral reefs

A **coral reef** is a beautiful sea garden. Many wonderful plants, animals, and fish live on and around it. The coral is built from the skeletons of tiny **coral polyps**. It forms fantastic shapes which can look like curly leaves, giant mushrooms, lacy fans, or tiny pipes.

A sea garden

The living polyps are like orange, yellow, purple, or green flowers. Colorful starfish and **sea anemones** also live on the coral reef. Strange-looking tropical fish swim along it, searching for prey. They include beautiful angel fish, striped spiny lionfish, and tiny sea horses.

Tiny tubes

Coral polyps, the animals who build the coral, are like little cylinders. They have a mouth at one end surrounded by tiny, waving **tentacles**. Polyps live tightly packed together in groups called **colonies**.

Animal builders

The coral polyp's skeleton grows outside its body. It forms when the polyp takes in small particles of a **mineral** called **calcium** from the seawater. The calcium changes inside the polyp's body and is squeezed out to form the coral. As each new polyp grows, the coral reef also gets bigger.

The dramatic colors of a coral reef.

Animals

WHAT YOU NEED

cardboard box

tissue paper

wire

sand

shells

peach pits

sponge

silver foil

tape

paint brush

paints

sequins

glue

Coral box

Stick seashells to the outside of your coral box

1 Rip strips of different colored tissue paper. Glue in enough strips to cover the inside of the box.

2 Cut the sponges into coral shapes and decorate them with sequins and paint.

3 Twist strips of silver foil and tissue paper together. Glue to the roof of the box so they hang down to the floor.

5 Paint the peach pits. Make fins from tissue paper, glue to each end of a pit and decorate with sequins.

4 Glue the sponges inside the box. Cover the base of the box with glue and sprinkle sand on top.

6 Wrap wire around your fish.

Poke small holes in the top of the box, thread the wire through and tape the ends. Hang the fish at different heights.

Fins and flippers

All swimming animals have fins or flippers so they can balance and push themselves through the water. Fish have only fins and penguins have only flippers. But dolphins, whales, and seals have both. Sea turtles, ducks, and sea gulls use their webbed feet like flippers, to paddle and steer through the water.

Flip-flops

Dolphins, whales, and seals are sea animals with flippers in place of legs. The powerful tail fins of dolphins and whales move them forward through the water. All dolphins and some whales also have a fin on top of their body, which keeps them upright in the water. Seals belong to the animal family called **pinnipeds**, which means "fin-footed." A seal's four swimming "legs" are more like flippers than fins. Seals live on land as well as in the sea, but they move awkwardly on land. They shuffle from place to place, using their powerful stomach muscles and their flippers to help them along.

Underwater flyers

Penguins are birds with flippers instead of wings. They are excellent swimmers, flying through the water in the same way that birds fly through the air. They swim underwater at a speed of about eight miles per hour (13 km/h) and come up to breathe once a minute. Penguins are also expert divers, plunging as deep as 900 feet (274 m) below the sea's surface.

Fishy fins

Most fish have fins on top, underneath, and on either side of their bodies. These help them to balance and to steer. Strong tail fins propel the fish forward. Fast-swimming sharks have about eight large, triangular fins, including a powerful tail fin, a single back fin, and several side fins.

A colony of Northern fur seals.

Animals

Dolphin sculpture

WHAT YOU NEED

clay

stones

paints and brush

glitter

stick

PVA glue

1 Divide the clay into two balls and roll between your hands to soften it.

2 Create a dolphin shape with one ball of clay and a rock shape with the other.

3 Make a hole in the top of the rock with the stick. The hole needs to be deep enough for the stick to stand up in it.

4 Push the top of the stick into the belly of the dolphin. Remove it once a hole has been made. Leave to dry.

Varnish your sculpture with PVA glue mixed with water.

5 Paint the dolphin and rock. Add glitter to make them shimmer.

Stand the stick in the rock and place the dolphin on top of it. Scatter stones around the base.

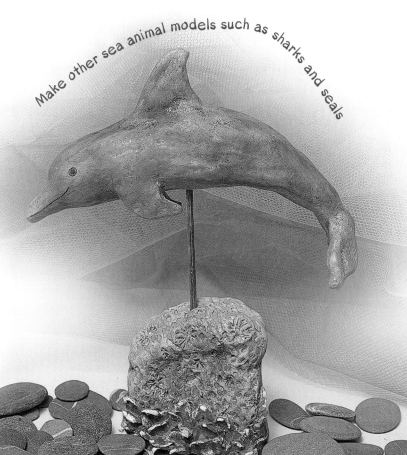

Make other sea animal models such as sharks and seals

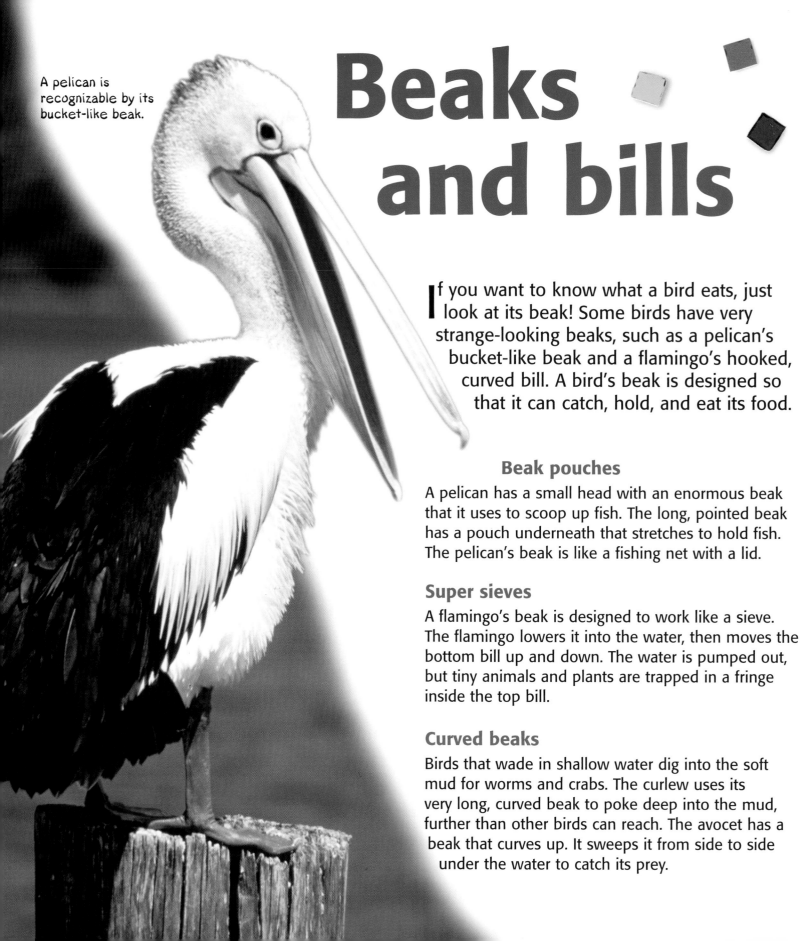

A pelican is recognizable by its bucket-like beak.

Beaks and bills

If you want to know what a bird eats, just look at its beak! Some birds have very strange-looking beaks, such as a pelican's bucket-like beak and a flamingo's hooked, curved bill. A bird's beak is designed so that it can catch, hold, and eat its food.

Beak pouches

A pelican has a small head with an enormous beak that it uses to scoop up fish. The long, pointed beak has a pouch underneath that stretches to hold fish. The pelican's beak is like a fishing net with a lid.

Super sieves

A flamingo's beak is designed to work like a sieve. The flamingo lowers it into the water, then moves the bottom bill up and down. The water is pumped out, but tiny animals and plants are trapped in a fringe inside the top bill.

Curved beaks

Birds that wade in shallow water dig into the soft mud for worms and crabs. The curlew uses its very long, curved beak to poke deep into the mud, further than other birds can reach. The avocet has a beak that curves up. It sweeps it from side to side under the water to catch its prey.

Animals

Floating duck

1

Cut a plastic bottle in half and stuff it with newspaper. Glue the toilet roll on top of the open end of the bottle to make the head and stuff it with newspaper.

2 Create wings by drawing shapes on poster board and cutting them out. Glue the wings onto each side of your duck.

Make a family of ducks for your bathroom

3 Cut a piece of poster board in the shape of a beak. Tape it to the front of the duck's head.

4 Cover the whole duck with glue and stick on strips of newspaper.

5 When dry, paint your duck.

Finally, give your duck a coat of varnish to make it waterproof!

Feathers

J ust as we wear clothes to keep warm, a bird wears feathers. These grow out of its skin and have many uses. They keep the bird warm and dry, they allow it to fly, they protect it from bumps and bruises – and they help the bird to blend in with its surroundings, so it can hide from predators.

Clean feathers

Birds spend several hours a day combing, or **preening**, their feathers with their beaks and feet. Feathers need to be kept clean in order to work properly. A small bird, such as a wren, has about 5,000 feathers. Larger birds, such as owls, have more than 10,000 feathers. A very large bird, such as a swan or an eagle, has more than 20,000 feathers.

Wing tips and tail feathers

Flight feathers are attached to the bird's wings and tail. These are broad, flat, and stiff, so they can push through the air when flying. An owl's flight feathers have very soft, furry edges that hardly make a sound as they swish through the air, so it can swoop down silently on its prey. A kestrel shivers its wings instead of flapping them, so that it can hover in one place, like a helicopter. Most birds fan out their wing tips and tail feathers, which work like brakes, slowing them down as they land.

Feathery patterns

The patterns and colors on some feathers help birds to blend in with their surroundings. The white feathers of a snowy owl, for example, blend in with the icy landscape of its **Arctic** home. Owls that live in forests, such as the tawny owl, are speckled brown so they can hide among twigs and branches.

Brand-new plumage

Once or twice each year, a bird grows new feathers to replace the old, worn ones. The new feathers grow quickly from the skin as the unwanted ones molt, or fall out. For a few days, the bird looks messy, but soon it has a bright new set of feathers, or plumage, and is ready to fly again.

Animals

WHAT YOU NEED

feathers

beads

wire

black string

Feathery necklace

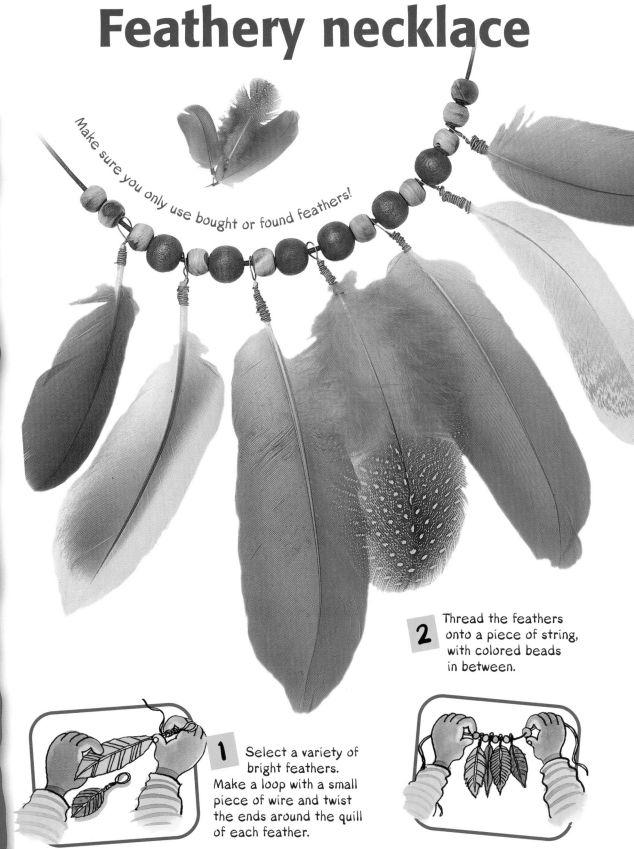

Make sure you only use bought or found feathers!

2 Thread the feathers onto a piece of string, with colored beads in between.

1 Select a variety of bright feathers. Make a loop with a small piece of wire and twist the ends around the quill of each feather.

All kinds of shells

Many animals that live in the sea make their own "houses" in the form of shells. These animals are called shellfish. The shell develops from a soft skin around the animal's body organs and protects the animal inside. Clams and oysters are examples of shellfish.

Bivalves

A shellfish with two shells joined together by a hinge is called a bivalve. When the shells are open, water can be let in and out through two tubes. Bivalves come in different shapes and sizes. They include oysters, scallops, mussels, cockles, and clams.

Giant clam

The giant clam is the biggest bivalve of all. It can grow to 53 inches (135 cm) in length and live for hundreds of years. During the day, the clam opens to allow light in. Algae living inside the clam use the light to make food. The algae and clam depend on one another to live.

Body protection

Many animals without backbones, called **invertebrates**, grow shells. These are made of a hard substance called **chitin**. Some shells are part of the animal's body and grow with the animal. Other shells are rigid, which means that they do not grow and are shed, then replaced by a larger shell.

Seashell paperweight

filler paste

bowl

large stone

paintbrush

wooden spoon

shells and small stones

poster board

scissors

paints

You can also decorate with beads, sequins, glitter, or colored stones

1 Mix the filler according to the instructions on the package.

Spread the filler thickly over the top of the stone.

2

3 Arrange the shells and stones by pressing them into the filler in a pattern.

4 When dry, paint the rest of your paperweight.

Make a picture frame

Use a piece of poster board to make the frame. You can cut the poster board into any shape you like. Then cut a rectangular hole in the middle, slightly smaller than the picture you wish to frame. Now follow steps 1 to 4 above to decorate your picture frame.

Light and dark

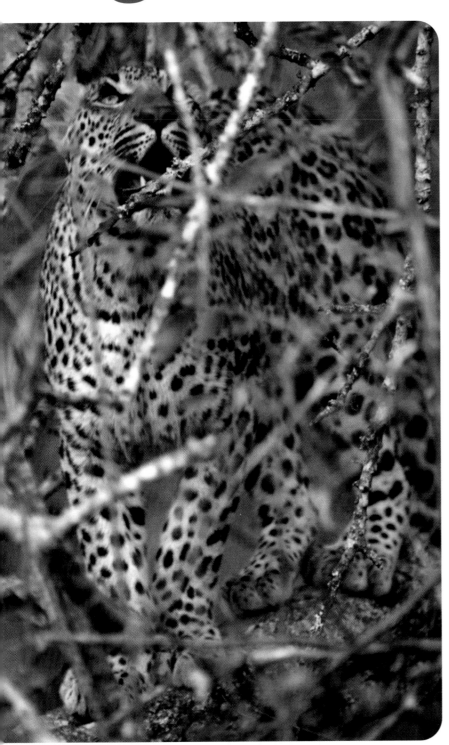

Many hunting animals have coats that are patterned or colored so that they blend in with their surroundings. This coloring is called camouflage. Camouflage helps an animal to stay hidden while **stalking** its prey. Leopards hide unseen in thorn trees, where their spotted coats blend in with the branches. Once they have made a kill, leopards often drag their prey back into the tree to eat.

Shadows in the dark

It can be dark on the floor of a rainforest, even during the day. Not much sunlight falls through the thick clusters of leaves and branches. In the gloom, a prowling animal may look just like a moving shadow. Some rainforest animals have such dark coats that at night only their eyes can be seen. The black panther's dark fur is covered with black spots, so that it easily blends into the forest at night.

White light

In the freezing Arctic, many animals have white fur which blends in with the snow around them. The large polar bear is difficult to see against the white landscape, so it can easily catch its prey. Every winter, the Arctic fox grows a coat of white fur, so it can stay hidden in the snow. When the snow melts in summer and uncovers the rough ground, the Arctic fox turns brown again and can still move around unseen.

Animals

Panther on the prowl...

WHAT YOU NEED

white pencil

black and white paper

scissors

gluestick

black tissue paper

Make creeping shadow pictures of all kinds of jungle animals

2 Glue the panther shape onto a piece of white paper. Turn the paper over.

3 Tear strips of black tissue paper and glue them over the prowling panther, like a screen.

1 Draw an outline of a prowling panther on a piece of black paper and cut it out.

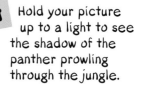

4 Hold your picture up to a light to see the shadow of the panther prowling through the jungle.

Add some jungle vines to your picture

You could stick your picture on the window

43

In disguise

Danger lurks deep in the rainforest! A hungry predator is waiting to pounce at every turn. The smaller rainforest animals must defend themselves in whatever way they can. Many of them use camouflage for protection. It helps them to blend in with the background, so they are hard to see. Some animals are even **disguised** as something else.

Toad leaves

Many animals rely on their natural skin patterns and coloring in order to blend in with their surroundings. An animal's skin coloring often reflects where it lives. Horned toads live on the rainforest floor. They are also called leaf litter toads. This is because their bodies are the same color as the dead leaves that have fallen to the ground. When a predator comes prowling, the toad defends itself by sitting very still among the leaves.

Invisible animals

Green tree frogs live in the trees, but it is very hard to see their bright-green bodies among the leaves. Other rainforest frogs can turn green, brown, or red to match their surroundings. Snakes, such as the tree boa, have **mottled** skin patterns that blend perfectly with their forest environment. A snake can also disguise its long, thin shape by coiling itself around the branches of trees. Green vine snakes, for example, look just like hanging vines.

In disguise

Some small animals are disguised as other animals or objects. Stick insects look exactly like twigs to fool hungry birds or foraging bush pigs. Leaf katydids look like grasshoppers and live in bushes and shrubs close to the ground. Their bodies are shaped like a crumpled leaf that has fallen from a tree. Few predators find dead leaves tasty, so the leaf katydids are safe. Other animals mimic, or pretend to be, animals that are dangerous or bad tasting. There is even a moth caterpillar that looks like a snake!

Index

47

M

The crafts
products
cannot locat
with those v
the craft wit

Gold foil: ca
sometime

Silver foil: ca
sometimes
substituted
harder fini

PVA glue: cor
creates a t
strong glue
and used a

Filler paste: s
when it dri

Paste: a paste
warm wate
mâché craf
mixed as p

Cellophane: a
used in craf
thin plastic

GROW YOUR MIND

BOOST
YOUR
BRAIN

Written by Alice Harman
Illustrated by David Broadbent

CRABTREE
PUBLISHING COMPANY
WWW.CRABTREEBOOKS.COM

CRABTREE
PUBLISHING COMPANY
WWW.CRABTREEBOOKS.COM

Author: Alice Harman
Series designer: David Broadbent
Illustrator: David Broadbent
Editor: Crystal Sikkens
Proofreader: Melissa Boyce
Print coordinator: Katherine Berti

A trusted adult is a person (over 18 years old) in a child's life who makes them feel safe, comfortable, and supported. It might be a parent, teacher, family friend, social worker, or another adult.

Library and Archives Canada Cataloguing in Publication

Title: Boost your brain / written by Alice Harman ; illustrated by David Broadbent.
Names: Harman, Alice, author. | Broadbent, David, 1977- illustrator.
Description: Series statement: Grow your mind | Includes index. | First published in Great Britain in 2020 by the Watts Publishing Group.
Identifiers: Canadiana (print) 2020021988X | Canadiana (ebook) 20200219936 | ISBN 9780778781660 (hardcover) | ISBN 9780778781745 (softcover) | ISBN 9781427125927 (HTML)
Subjects: LCSH: Brain—Care and hygiene—Juvenile literature. | LCSH: Brain—Growth—Juvenile literature. | LCSH: Mental health—Juvenile literature. | LCSH: Thought and thinking—Juvenile literature.
Classification: LCC QP376 .H37 2021 | DDC j612.8/2—dc23

Library of Congress Cataloging-in-Publication Data

Names: Harman, Alice, author. | Broadbent, David, 1977- illustrator.
Title: Boost your brain / written by Alice Harman ; illustrated by David Broadbent.
Description: New York : Crabtree Publishing Company, 2021. | Series: Grow your mind | Includes index.
Identifiers: LCCN 2020014727 (print) | LCCN 2020014728 (ebook) | ISBN 9780778781660 (hardcover) | ISBN 9780778781745 (paperback) | ISBN 9781427125927 (ebook)
Subjects: LCSH: Mental efficiency--Juvenile literature. | Intellect--Juvenile literature. | Brain--Juvenile literature.
Classification: LCC BF431 .H34195 2021 (print) | LCC BF431 (ebook) | DDC 155.4/191--dc23
LC record available at https://lccn.loc.gov/2020014727
LC ebook record available at https://lccn.loc.gov/2020014728

Crabtree Publishing Company
www.crabtreebooks.com   1-800-387-7650
Published by Crabtree Publishing Company in 2021

Published in Canada
Crabtree Publishing
616 Welland Ave.
St. Catharines, Ontario
L2M 5V6

Published in the United States
Crabtree Publishing
347 Fifth Ave.
Suite 1402-145
New York, NY 10116

Printed in the U.S.A./082020/CG20200601

First published in Great Britain in 2020 by The Watts Publishing Group Copyright © The Watts Publishing Group 2020

CONTENTS

A brain-boosting mindset

"I'm not smart enough to do that, there's no point trying."

"Argh, I just don't understand this! I'll never get it."

"Everything's easy for her because she's smarter than me."

Have you ever had any of these thoughts? How did they make you feel? Not great, right?

Sometimes we think about our brains as if they are stuck one way forever. We believe we can either do something or we can't, we're either smart or we're not. This way of thinking is known as a **fixed mindset**, and none of it is true!

The best way to boost our brains is to develop a **growth mindset**. This means understanding that the brain is never fixed as it is. We always have the power to make it change and grow.

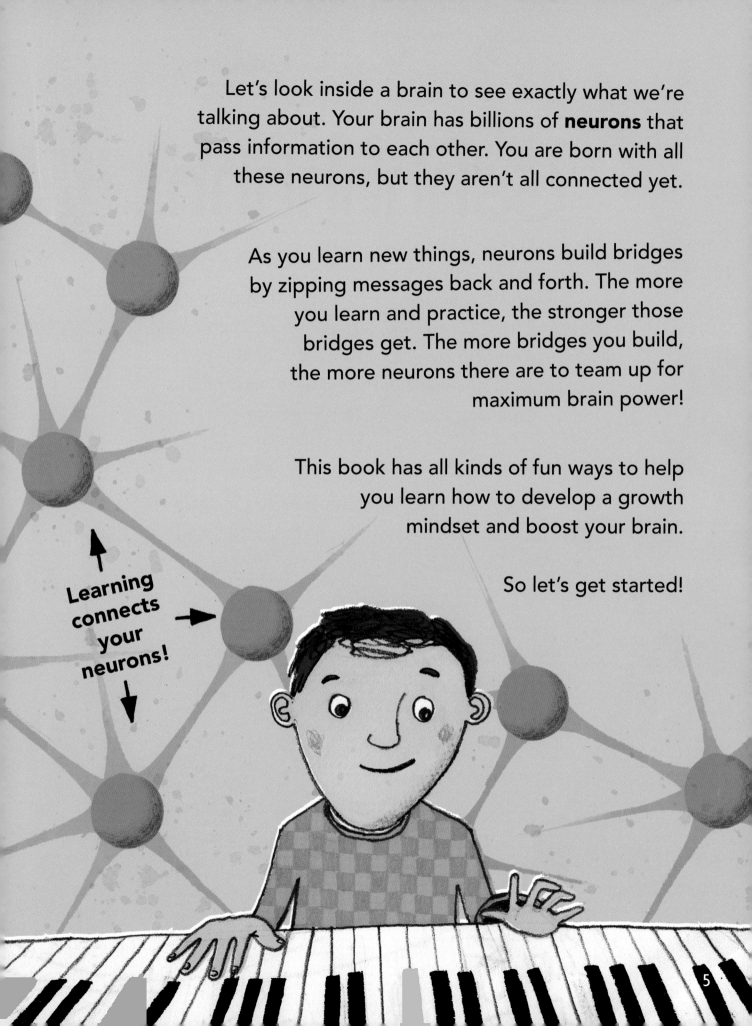

Let's look inside a brain to see exactly what we're talking about. Your brain has billions of **neurons** that pass information to each other. You are born with all these neurons, but they aren't all connected yet.

As you learn new things, neurons build bridges by zipping messages back and forth. The more you learn and practice, the stronger those bridges get. The more bridges you build, the more neurons there are to team up for maximum brain power!

This book has all kinds of fun ways to help you learn how to develop a growth mindset and boost your brain.

So let's get started!

Learning connects your neurons!

Sshhhhhhh...

Friends trying to talk to you, thoughts
popping into your head, situations you can't help
worrying about... Do you ever feel like your
brain is so crowded with thoughts and noises
that you just can't think properly?

Well, you're right! It's really hard for your brain to
do its best work when it's so distracted and
overloaded by all these other things.

You can boost your brain power by finding ways
to take away these distractions, so you
have a clear mind to focus on
whatever you're trying to do.

Jamal

I was finding it really hard to concentrate in class. My friends kept talking to me when I was trying to listen or do my work.

It felt like there wasn't enough time to think in between people distracting me, so I was struggling to understand things.

I talked to my dad about it. We decided that I would tell my friends that although I loved talking to them, I needed to stop talking in class so I could focus more on my work.

They were really nice about it, but my friend Anna kept forgetting. I had to remind her to please stop talking to me in class, and that was really hard! But now I feel much happier and we're all still really good friends!

7

One thing at a time

Do you feel your mind wandering when you're trying to concentrate? Are you thinking about what you're going to have for dinner, what you're doing on the weekend, or what the words are to your new favorite song?

Even without people distracting you, it can be really tricky to focus on one thing for a long time—or even for a short time!

Your brain needs to concentrate on new challenges to make connections and grow, so how can you help it?

Well, just like a weight lifter strengthens their muscles over time, you can boost your brain by building up its concentration power bit by bit.

Try

Find an apple, then start a timer for 30 seconds and stare at the apple until the timer beeps. Try not to think about anything else but this apple during that time. It's harder than you think!

Think

How did that go? You may have found that other thoughts popped into your head and that's completely normal. When this happens, it can be helpful to say to yourself, "Oh, there's a thought!" and then imagine pushing it away gently, so it floats off like a balloon. You can also try focusing on counting to four as you breathe in, and then again as you breathe out. Silently saying "apple" over and over again to yourself is another trick to try.

Practice

Try it for 30 seconds again tomorrow. Then, in a notebook, write down the date, the length of time—"30 seconds," and a couple of lines about how it went. The next day, try 40 seconds, then 50, and so on. At the end of two weeks, look back and see how you've progressed and what you found that helped you focus best—you're the expert on your own brain!

Think, rest, repeat

We all want to do our best, but sometimes we need to remember that we are human beings, not machines.

Human beings can't keep working at top speed with maximum focus forever—our brains need a break!

If you've been working on something for a long time and you're getting frustrated because it's not going as well as you'd like, take a break. It's very hard for your brain to do its best thinking and growing when it's tired.

Taking regular rest breaks will boost your brain, leaving it happy and ready to learn for longer periods of time.

The next time you have a big project or a lot of homework to do, try splitting it up into sections with breaks in between.

Set a timer for 15 minutes when you start one section of work.

When it goes off, set the timer again for five minutes and take a break. During each break, think of a different way to do these three things:

1. Move around

2. Make yourself smile

3. Say something nice to yourself

When the break timer goes off, start the next section of work and set the timer again.

After three five-minute breaks, if you really need to keep working, give yourself a longer break.

Brain hugs

Do you ever say horrible, mean things to yourself that you'd never dream of saying to your friends?

Sometimes we can be really hard on ourselves, and it hurts our brains when we think like this. It stops them from doing their best learning and growing.

Think about it like this: if someone was really mean to you, and told you there was no point in trying because you wouldn't do it right anyway, would you still want to try? Probably not.

So we need to learn how to turn these mean, negative thoughts into friendly, positive **brain hugs!**

Jess

When I started playing soccer I really liked it,
but after a while I felt like everyone else was
better than me and it made me really upset.

I told myself that no one wanted me there, that I was
no good, and I was ruining it for everyone else. I was
thinking about quitting, even though it was still fun.

I talked to my uncle about it and he was really shocked. He
thought I was so brave for joining the team even though I didn't
know anyone there, and it sounded like I was learning a lot.

The next time I went to soccer, I tried to remember these
positive things and it made me feel so much better.
Now I'm really enjoying it again, and getting better
all the time. Whenever I start feeling bad, I just
give myself a "brain hug" and it really helps!

Time-out

When we get really worried, angry, confused,
or frustrated, it can feel like we're trapped in
that feeling and nothing can change that.

We might do things that we know aren't right and will
make us feel bad later, such as cheating on a test or
being mean to a friend we think has everything easy.

At these times, the best way to make a good decision
is to give your brain a chance to calm down first. Take
a time-out, breathe, and try to get yourself back in the
right frame of mind to handle whatever is going on.

1.
Everyone's brain works a little differently, so let's create a **mind map** with the best ways to help yours calm down when you feel stuck or panicky.

2.
Draw your brain in the middle of a piece of paper. Add the different things that help you feel calm. They could be counting to 100, taking some deep breaths, or maybe remembering a happy time.

4.
Practice the different time-outs on your mind map, so you can remember them easily when you need them.

3.
Ask your family and friends what helps them to calm down, and maybe try out some of these ideas. If they work for you, add them to your mind map.

Take care of your body

Your brain is a funny and special thing because it's your mind and your body at the same time!

Sometimes we think about the "mind" side of our brain so much, such as our thoughts and feelings, that we forget to take care of the "body" side of it.

You can boost your brain by taking care of yourself in simple ways every day:

Drink up

Your brain cells need the right balance of water. If you get too thirsty, they don't work as well.

Get moving

Your brain loves exercise and you should do an hour of it every day. When your heart beats faster from running, jumping, swimming, and so on, it sends more oxygen to your brain and gives it a big boost.

Brain food

Stay healthy and boost your brain by eating a rainbow of different-colored fresh foods, including berries, beans, apples, and plums. Avoid too many sweets and sugary drinks. After a rush of energy, these sweets will cause you to have a sugar crash, which makes your body and brain suddenly feel tired.

Sleep tight

Try to get nine to twelve hours of sleep every night, or your brain will be tired and you'll feel it! If you have to get up early for school, count back the hours from when you have to wake up, to make sure you get to bed early enough.

BRAIN DUMP

Does your brain ever feel completely overloaded with all the different things you have to remember? Does it feel like there's no space left in it to think?

You can boost your brain by using a notebook to unload some of the thoughts it's trying to juggle. This frees up your brain to focus all its power on what it's doing at that moment.

We ask a LOT of our brains every day. It can be like trying to juggle many balls at the same time—we're so busy trying not to let anything fall that we can't do anything else. And it really drains our energy through the day.

Ask an adult to help you write a schedule
in a notebook of what you do every day,
such as school, activities, clubs, and so on.

Write reminders in your schedule for anything that
you need to remember to do at certain times—
for example, pack your schoolbag in the morning.

Carry this notebook with you so you can always check it.
When something comes up that you need to remember
to do, such as give your parents or guardians a letter
from school, write it down.

Pick a time every evening where you take 15 minutes to look
over what you wrote down that day and what's coming up in
the day ahead. If there are any changes to your schedule,
add a sticky note to remind yourself.

PICTURE THIS

Have you ever felt like you knew or understood something, but then it disappeared out of your brain or stopped making sense later on? Don't worry, it's frustrating but it happens to everyone!

One thing that can really help with remembering new information is to visualize it. That means creating a picture in your mind of what you've just learned.

You can then draw that picture and keep it to look at later, along with notes you've written down. You could even try testing yourself by recreating the picture in your mind at a later date and then trying to draw it again. Compare it to the original drawing. How much did you remember?

Rekah

I felt really frustrated at school because I just couldn't remember things! I understood the lessons, but as soon as I learned them it felt like the facts fell out of my brain just like water through a sieve.

I told my teacher and she suggested that I try visualizing things as I learned them. I gave it a try that evening with my homework as I learned about different types of animals.

I learned that amphibians, such as frogs, are cold-blooded and live in water and on land. To remember this, I pictured a cold, shivering frog half-in and half-out of a pond.

In class the next day, my teacher asked us about amphibians. I pictured the cold, shivering frog in my mind and told her all the facts I remembered. She was so happy that I tried out a new way to boost my brain!

SUM IT UP

When you get to the end of a project or task, it can be tempting to want to take a well-deserved rest. And no one is saying you shouldn't! But before you do, give your brain a boost!

Spend one minute thinking about what you've just done. It can help you better understand how your brain works, and recognize patterns that might be causing you problems.

What did you learn?

How difficult did you find it?

How much effort did you put into it?

How happy are you with it?

What did you enjoy/ not enjoy about it?

What would you do differently next time?

Read through the questions on the previous page again.

Next time you finish a task or project, imagine that a crowd of news reporters is asking you all about it. Record yourself giving answers to all their questions.

One of the news reporters wants to film a full-length story all about you, so now they're following you around all week! Film yourself answering the same questions after every task or project you complete.

At the end of the week, watch the videos and make note of what you've said. Does anything keep coming up in each video?

Make a video finale where you talk about what you've learned and how you're going to try to work on any challenges.

Make a mnemonic

Boosting your brain doesn't have to be super-serious—it can be a lot of silly fun! One of the best ways to remember things is to make **mnemonics** (nuh-mon-ics).

That looks like a tricky word, doesn't it? But all it means is a way to help you remember information. You can use a mnemonic for anything, from science to spelling. Mnemonics can come in many forms, such as patterns of letters or numbers, rhymes, jokes, or songs.

Mnemonics that are funny or related to your life are the easiest to remember. Why not try making one right now for a word you find tricky to spell, such as mnemonics? One example for this word could be **M**y **N**eighbor **E**d **M**akes **O**dd, **N**ot **I**nteresting **C**at **S**ongs.

Marek

I love writing stories, but I find spelling is hard.
I used to hate seeing the spelling mistakes I made
when my teacher marked my work. It almost made
me want to stop writing stories all together.

I asked my dad how he remembered how to spell so many words.
He told me that when he got stuck on a word, he liked to use
a fun saying or a silly song to help him remember.

He shared one with me that he used for the word "because."
It went **B**ig **E**lephants **C**an **A**lways **U**nderstand **S**mall **E**lephants.
He told me to picture little elephants talking and big elephants
nodding along. Then we practiced writing down the word
with its correct spelling. It worked!

We've come up with other mnemonics for all kinds of words—
sometimes we even make up songs! It's really helped me feel
more confident with my spelling and writing.

Also, it's fun!

STUDY BUDDIES

Have you ever felt bad because you thought someone else was smarter than you? Have you felt good when you thought you were smarter than someone else?

Tests and competitions can sometimes make us feel like we're only doing well if we're beating everyone else, but this isn't right at all.

Wanting to prove we're the smartest can make us scared to make mistakes or ask for help. Feeling like we're not the smartest can stop us from wanting to try at all. Either way, it's not helpful for your brain!

Instead of competing against people, try boosting your brain by working together with others and learning from them.

Ask someone in your class to partner up with you on a project or to be study buddies in a subject that you are finding difficult.

Pick regular times to meet and work together. At the end of each study session, tell each other:

 one way you feel you're trying hard and improving;

 one way you can see them trying hard and improving;

★ **one thing you've learned from them.**

Brainy book

Everyone's brain is different and that's
what makes the world interesting!

You're the world's greatest expert when it comes
to your brain. You're going to be together for your
whole life, so it's a good idea to get to know what
keeps it growing and happy.

You may find that some of the ideas and
activities in this book work really well for
you, but others may not be helpful at all.
That's OK!

Turn a notebook into your own Brain Booster Journal. Use it to keep practicing the activities in this book that work well for you, and try out some new ideas of your own!

Keep track of your progress, so if you ever feel frustrated you can look back at your journal and see how far you've come and how much you've learned.

Remember that your brain needs time to change and grow. It might take a while before your new habits and ways of thinking feel natural, but if you keep putting in the effort, you will see the results.

Happy brain boosting!

KEEP BOOSTING YOUR BRAIN!

Read through this book's brain-boosting tips any time you need a quick reminder!

Try to remove distractions that stop your brain from being able to focus properly.

Practice thinking about one thing at a time to help build up your concentration power.

Give yourself regular rest breaks to keep your brain happy and working well.

Turn negative, mean thoughts about yourself into friendly, positive "brain hugs."

Work out what calms down your brain when you feel stuck and panicky.

Take care of your brain by getting plenty of sleep, exercising, eating healthy foods, and drinking water.

Free up some thinking space in your brain by writing down plans, reminders, and things to do.

Visualize new information as you learn it to help it stick in your brain.

Think about how you work and learn so you know what works best for you.

Try making up mnemonics to help you remember how to spell words or other pieces of information.

Work with others and learn from them rather than competing against them.

Become an expert in what makes your brain work best and be happiest.

Glossary

brain hug When you turn a nasty, negative thought about yourself into a positive, caring one that helps you and your brain feel better

fixed mindset If you are using a fixed mindset, you believe that your intelligence is fixed and can't be changed

growth mindset If you are using a growth mindset, you believe that your intelligence is always changing because your brain can grow stronger

mind map A diagram with lines and circles for organizing information so that it is easier to remember

mnemonic A rhyme, joke, or saying that helps a person remember something, from how to spell a word to the planets in our solar system

neurons Cells in your brain that pass information back and forth to each other

Index

Notes for adults

The concept of a "growth mindset" was developed by psychologist Carol Dweck, and is used to describe a way in which effective learners view themselves as being on a constant journey to develop their intelligence. This is supported by studies showing how our brains continue to develop throughout our lives, rather than intelligence and ability being static.

Responding with a growth mindset means being eager to learn more and seeing that making mistakes and getting feedback about how to improve are important parts of that journey.

A growth mindset is at one end of a continuum, and learners move between this and a "fixed mindset"—which is based on the belief that you're either smart or you're not.

A fixed mindset is unhelpful because it can make learners feel they need to "prove" rather than develop their intelligence. They may avoid challenges, not wanting to risk failing at anything, and this reluctance to make mistakes—and learn from them—can negatively affect the learning process.

Help children develop a growth mindset by:

• Giving specific positive feedback on their learning efforts, such as "Well done, you've been practicing…" rather than non-specific praise, such as "Good effort" or comments such as "Smart girl/boy!" that can encourage fixed-mindset thinking.

• Sharing times when you have had to persevere learning something new and what helped you succeed.

• Encouraging them to keep a learning journal, where they can explore what they learned from new challenges and experiences.

• Exploring the science behind how our brains work and change, watching online video clips that show the brain in neuron-firing action.